# BUDDHISM

## GLOBAL CITIZENS: WORLD RELIGIONS

Published in the United States of America by Cherry Lake Publishing
Ann Arbor, Michigan
www.cherrylakepublishing.com

Content Adviser: April C. Armstrong, Princeton University

Reading Adviser: Marla Conn MS, Ed., Literacy specialist, Read-Ability, Inc.

Photo Credits: © Bule Sky Studio/Shutterstock, cover, 1; © Fabio Imhoff/Shutterstock, 5; © Nadezhda1906/Shutterstock, 6; © Photographee.eu/Shutterstock, 8; © Dragon Images/Shutterstock, 10; © Globe Turner/Shutterstock, 13; © Sean Pavone/Shutterstock, 14; © Stephane Bidouze/Shutterstock, 16, 19; © Laura PI/Shutterstock, 20; © thodonal88/Shutterstock, 22; © vipflash/Shutterstock, 23; © beibaoke/Shutterstock, 25; © Gastuner/Shutterstock, 26; © mai111/Shutterstock, 28

Library of Congress Cataloging-in-Publication Data
Names: Marsico, Katie, 1980- author.
Title: Buddhism / by Katie Marsico.
Description: Ann Arbor, Michigan : Cherry Lake Publishing, 2017. | Series:
  Global citizens: world religions | Includes bibliographical references and index.
Identifiers: LCCN 2016033581 | ISBN 9781634721585 (hardcover) | ISBN 9781634722247 (pdf) |
  ISBN 9781634722902 (pbk.) | ISBN 9781634723565 (ebook)
Subjects: LCSH: Buddhism—Juvenile literature.
Classification: LCC BQ4032 .M375 2017 | DDC 294.3—dc23
LC record available at https://lccn.loc.gov/2016033581

Cherry Lake Publishing would like to acknowledge the work of the Partnership for 21st Century Learning.
Please visit www.p21.org for more information.

Printed in the United States of America
Corporate Graphics

## ABOUT THE AUTHOR

Katie Marsico is the author of more than 200 children's books. She lives in a suburb of Chicago, Illinois, with her husband and children.

# TABLE OF CONTENTS

# History: Roots of the Religion

Since people began recording history, they have written about the idea of a power greater than themselves. Thousands of years later, various beliefs in this power continue to shape both individual lives and entire cultures. Religion is the system people use to organize such beliefs. Religion also standardizes ceremonies and rules for worship.

## The Story of Siddhartha Gautama

Buddhism is an example of a major world religion. It is based on the idea that human suffering is part of a cycle of birth, death, and rebirth. Buddhists believe that gaining spiritual knowledge and awareness allows a person to break the cycle. Once someone reaches this point, he or she is said to have achieved

Siddhartha Gautama was the founder of Buddhism.

enlightenment. That individual is then able to enter nirvana, a state outside the cycle of death and rebirth, where the person is finally free from suffering.

Historians say the history of Buddhism can be traced back to the sixth century BCE. That is when Siddhartha Gautama was most likely born in India. He eventually became the founder of Buddhism.

Gautama was the son of a warrior-king and enjoyed great wealth and **nobility**. Yet, according to the story of how Buddhism developed, he decided to give up this lifestyle. One

Meditation is an important part of the Buddhist practice.

day, Gautama was touring a park outside his palace. He saw a sick person, an old person, a dead body, and a holy man. The first three were a reminder that all people experience suffering. The holy man stood out to Gautama for a different reason. He had a look of kindness, peace, and happiness on his face.

Gautama was amazed that—even when surrounded by sadness, pain, and death—the holy man had found **contentment**. Not long afterward, Gautama abandoned his life of luxury. Instead, he wandered in the wilderness for six years and denied himself any material comforts. He hoped that, like the holy man, he also would achieve enlightenment.

## Becoming "the Enlightened One"

During his journey, Gautama fasted, or didn't allow himself food and drink. He also meditated. The process of meditation is a mental exercise that involves thought and reflection. Gautama participated in these **rituals** to increase his spiritual awareness.

While meditating under a tree one night, Gautama finally accomplished his goal. By the time he awoke the next morning,

### Developing Questions

*Which parts of the Buddha's message appealed to his early followers? Why? What other religions already existed in India when Buddhism developed? How were they similar to—and different from—the Buddhist faith?*

*The first two questions are examples of compelling questions. Compelling questions don't have clear-cut answers but lead to interesting discussions and debates. The third and fourth questions are supporting questions. They have more specific answers. Supporting questions often help people form answers to compelling questions.*

Buddhists believe that helping other people brings you good karma.

he had achieved enlightenment! He suddenly understood all truths, as well as how to overcome human suffering. From that point forward, he became known as the Buddha, which is **Sanskrit** for the "enlightened one."

## Beliefs That the Buddha Shared

The Buddha proceeded to travel throughout India to share his spiritual knowledge with others. During his lessons, he talked about three marks, or signs, of existence. One was *anicca*—the idea that everything is always changing. Another was *dukkha*—

the idea that nothing in life is perfect, and even good things bring suffering when they are gone. The final mark was *anatta*—the idea that there is no self (soul), or inner spirit.

According to the Buddha, people had a life force called karma. Acting in a positive way led to good karma, while acting in a negative way caused bad karma. (Activities such as breathing and sleeping were said to produce neutral karma.)

The Buddha also declared that after death, people experienced rebirth. How they were reborn depended on their karma. People

## The Eight Parts of the Path

According to the Buddha's Eightfold Path, becoming wiser involves having right understanding, or acceptance of Buddhist marks and truths. Increased wisdom also requires right intention, or a commitment to learning the right attitudes and reasons for acting. To achieve **morality**, people need to have right speech, right action, and right livelihood. Their words, behavior, and work must encourage peace and harmony, versus fighting and pain. Finally, based on the Eightfold Path, effective meditation depends on right effort, right mindfulness, and right concentration. This means having a positive state of mind, awareness of one's body and feelings, and mental focus.

Buddhists believe the cause of suffering is wanting things.

with good karma were reborn into one of three favorable realms, or kingdoms. They returned as gods, **demigods**, or humans. Meanwhile, people with bad karma were reborn into one of three unfavorable realms. They came back as animals, ghosts, or beings trapped in hell. Only those individuals reborn into the realm of humans were able to escape this cycle and enter nirvana.

Another part of the Buddha's teachings focused on the Four Noble Truths. The first truth was that everyone experiences some sort of disappointment or suffering during their lifetime. The second truth was that desire causes suffering. The Buddha said people are constantly seeking things, which is why they suffer. The third truth was that learning how to end desire is the same as learning how to end suffering. The fourth truth was that it is indeed possible to get rid of desire—and suffering. To help people accomplish this goal, the Buddha advised them to follow the truths of the Eightfold Path. The Path described eight ways to gain wisdom, morality, and the ability to meditate.

# Geography: Mapping How Faith Formed

**G**autama died in the early fifth century BCE. By that time, however, Buddhism was already spreading. Communities of **monks** in northern India continued to share the Buddha's ideas about achieving enlightenment.

Buddhism grew beyond this region during the third century BCE. Under Emperor Ashoka, who then ruled the Indian subcontinent, it became the state religion. Buddhist **missionaries** brought the Buddha's teachings to southern India, as well as Sri Lanka. (The island of Sri Lanka is located in the Indian Ocean, off of India's southeastern coast.)

During Ashoka's reign, Buddhism even reached portions of Greece, Egypt, and Syria. Gradually, different forms of the religion

HOTAN

GOLMUD

AFGHANISTAN

KABUL

ISLAMABAD

LAHORE

CHINA

PAKISTAN

DELHI

NEW DELHI

JAIPUR

KANPUR

NEPAL

KATHMANDU

LHASA

THIMPHU

BHUTAN

HYDERABAD

KARACHI

PATNA

BANGLADESH

DHAKA

CHITTA

MAN

JABALPUR

VADODARA

KOLKATA
(CALCUTTA)

INDIA

MUMBAI
(BOMBAY)

NAY PY

MYA
(B

HYDERABAD

Bay
of
Bengal

Y
(RA

Arabian
Sea

BANGALORE

CHENNAI
(MADRAS)

Andaman Islands
(India)

Buddhism spread from India to Sri Lanka and other countries.

INDIAN OCEAN

SRI LANKA

COLOMBO

The Golden Pavilion is a Buddhist temple in Kyoto, Japan.

started to develop. Yet they were all based on the same basic beliefs that the Buddha had discussed with his earliest followers.

## Spreading Across Asia

Beginning in the first century CE, merchants and sailors introduced Buddhism to other parts of Southeast Asia. It gained popularity in what are present-day Myanmar, Thailand, Cambodia, and Laos. During the next several centuries, people also started practicing Buddhism in China, Korea, Japan, and Tibet.

Oddly enough, Buddhism didn't remain a major religion in India. Between the eighth and 10th centuries, it seemed to disappear from the very nation where it had formed. Most historians agree that religions such as Hinduism and Islam ultimately overshadowed Buddhism in India.

## Present Populations

Today, about 488 million people across the globe practice Buddhism. According to recent studies, Buddhists represent roughly 7 percent of the world's population. Almost 99 percent of

# Gathering and Evaluating Sources

*The earliest collection of Buddhist scriptures, or holy writings, are found within the Tripitaka. The Tripitaka is made up of three groups of books. The first, the Vinaya Pitaka, contains laws for Buddhist monks and nuns. The second, the Sutra Pitaka, features accounts of the Buddha's **sermons** and teachings. The third, the Abhidharma Pitaka, is a series of songs, poems, and stories. The Buddha's disciples, or followers, recorded the Tripitaka during the third century BCE. They wrote it in Pali—an ancient Indian language spoken between the sixth and second centuries BCE.*

Most Buddhists live in Asia.

these individuals live in Asia. The largest number of Buddhists are found in China, Thailand, Japan, and Myanmar. More than 392 million people there base their religious beliefs on the teachings of the Buddha. Meanwhile, Sri Lanka, Vietnam, Cambodia, South Korea, India, and Malaysia are home to nearly 68 million Buddhists.

Outside of the Asia-Pacific region, significant Buddhist populations mainly exist in North America and Europe. Buddhism is the religion of 3.9 million North Americans and 1.3 million Europeans. Finally, approximately 1.1 million people practice Buddhism in Central and South America, the Middle East, and sub-Saharan Africa.

# CHAPTER 3

# Civics: Organization and Ideas

There are many different forms of Buddhism. Yet most usually fit into one of two major subgroups, or sects. These are Theravada Buddhism and Mahayana Buddhism.

## Theravada Buddhism

In the Pali language, *Theravada* means "way of the elders." Theravada Buddhists trace their faith to the elders, or senior members, of the earliest community of Buddhist monks. People who practice this type of Buddhism think their way of life most closely reflects the Buddha's teachings.

In Theravada Buddhism, various gods are said to exist. Yet they are not all-powerful beings who control how humans live. Instead,

Theravada Buddhists believe that only holy people can reach nirvana.

Theravada Buddhists say every person is responsible for achieving his or her own enlightenment.

According to Theravada Buddhists, it is difficult for **laypeople** to become arhats, or people who have achieved enlightenment and reached nirvana. They consider it far easier for monks and nuns to escape the cycle of birth, death, and rebirth. Most believe that, at best, laypeople will die and be reborn as holy people. Theravada Buddhism is widely practiced among Buddhists in Sri Lanka, Cambodia, Thailand, Laos, and Myanmar.

Many Buddhists use mandalas (spiritual diagrams of the universe) in meditation.

## Mahayana Buddhism

Instead of focusing on arhats, Mahayana Buddhists are more concerned with the idea of bodhisattva. This term is Sanskrit for "enlightenment being." To Mahayana Buddhists, both laypeople and holy people are capable of becoming bodhisattvas. What's most important is that such individuals are selfless, work toward enlightenment, and try to help others achieve it.

In Mahayana Buddhism, it's not always necessary to experience rebirth for enlightenment to occur. Many Mahayana Buddhists say it's possible to reach nirvana within a single lifetime. Yet they believe it's often better to choose rebirth, rather than avoiding the cycle of death and rebirth. By allowing themselves to be reborn, Mahayana Buddhists hope to return and show others how to achieve enlightenment. Mahayana Buddhism has a strong influence in nations such as Tibet, China, Taiwan, Japan, Korea, and Mongolia.

## Where and How Worship Occurs

Buddhist rituals and traditions sometimes vary, depending on specific locations and subgroups. Temples, or houses of worship, range from towers called "pagodas" to dome-shaped buildings

## Developing Claims and Using Evidence

Why did early Buddhists feel the need to separate into the two main denominations you just read about? First, think about the distinctions, or differences, between both subgroups. Next, use this information to develop a statement that answers the question above. Then get ready to do some research online or at the library or local houses of worship. (Hint: Be cautious when reviewing online sources. Some are more reliable than others. Web sites operated by government agencies or colleges and universities are often good places to start.) As you gather evidence, find facts that support the ideas in your claim!

Burning incense is a Buddhist tradition.

known as "stupas." People who practice Buddhism also worship at home. They often set aside part of their living space as a shrine, or holy area.

Whether Buddhists worship in a temple or at a household shrine, they usually remove their shoes and hats first. This is done as a sign of respect. During worship, people generally face a statue or image of the Buddha. Candles, **incense**, and chanting are other common features.

When Buddhists chant, they repeat portions of their scripture in a rhythmic manner. Many also recite mantras. A mantra is a sound, word, or phrase that is said once or several times during prayer or meditation.

## Celebrating Faith

In Buddhism, several holidays and festivals serve as opportunities for people to celebrate their beliefs. Some of the main Buddhist holidays are described below.

| Holiday | When It's Celebrated | Main Theme |
|---------|---------------------|------------|
| Sangha Day | March | Festival celebrating the Buddhist community and recalling how 1,250 enlightened monks gathered to hear the Buddha's first sermon |
| Songkran | April | Festival where people visit family and splash one another with water for good luck |
| Vesak | May or June | Recalling the Buddha's birth (as Siddhartha Gautama), enlightenment, and entrance into nirvana |
| Madhu Purnima | August or September | Celebrating unity and charity by bringing honey to local shrines |

Note: Dates often vary, depending on the geographic location of individual faith communities and the practices within different denominations.

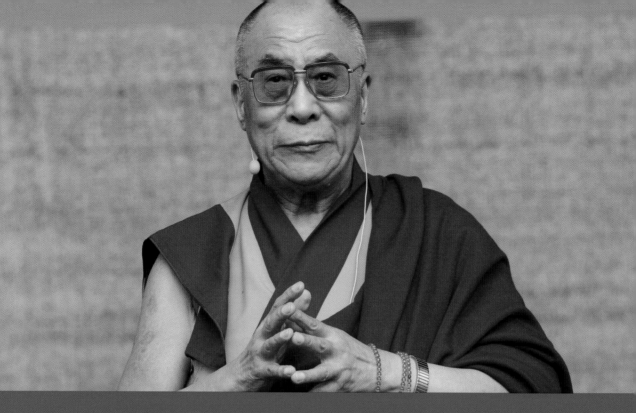

The Dalai Lama is the leader of Tibetan Buddhism.

# Vajrayana Buddhism

Vajrayana Buddhism is often viewed as a type of Mahayana Buddhism. It is most commonly practiced in Tibet, Nepal, Bhutan, and Mongolia. Vajrayana Buddhists perform certain rituals in the hopes of achieving enlightenment more quickly. These include meditation, **yoga**, and working with spiritual guides, or gurus. In Tibet, where Vajrayana Buddhism strongly influences local Buddhist populations, the term guru translates to "lama." The Dalai Lama is a world-famous religious figure and is considered the spiritual leader of Tibetan Buddhism.

# Economics: Funding a Faith

The Buddha taught that the desire for material wealth leads to suffering. The earliest Buddhist monks were homeless. They owned just their robes and a begging bowl. Laypeople placed **alms** in the monks' bowls as they traveled from village to village. These gifts of food prevented the holy men from going hungry.

Today, monks in areas such as Thailand still beg for alms. Yet food is only one basic need that modern Buddhists must address. They also have to find ways to meet the costs of building and caring for temples. Money is also needed to pay the salaries of people who work in Buddhist houses of worship.

Buddhist faith communities oversee several organizations that help people who are struggling. Some offer medical services in

Local people give the monks food each day.

regions affected by natural disaster. Others build schools or operate programs for children living with disabilities.

## Examples of Income

Buddhists often help their temples through pledges, or promises to donate a specific amount of money. In some cases, temples make appeals, or requests, for donations from their members on religious holidays. Some Buddhists also set aside money in their wills. They arrange for these funds to be given to Buddhist temples and charities following their death. Charitable organizations depend on

Many Buddhists donate money to the temples they attend.

# Communicating Conclusions

*Consider how Buddhists' beliefs help them perform a wide variety of charity work. Try to find out more about the services that different religious communities and organizations offer. (Hint: Think about contacting local temples and churches for additional information.) Do the ideas that shape most major world religions support giving back to others? Discuss your conclusions with friends and family. Or, if you practice an organized religion, share your observations with members of your faith community!*

volunteers, too. Many Buddhists share their time, skills, and knowledge to improve other peoples' lives.

## Inspired by Spiritual Awareness

The people who practice Buddhism are constantly trying to achieve greater spiritual awareness. As they work toward increased understanding and an end to suffering, Buddhists believe they grow closer to enlightenment. This belief was at the center of the Buddha's teachings roughly 2,500 years ago. It remains the focus of Buddhism today—and will inspire Buddhists for thousands of years to come.

## Taking Informed Action

*Before reading this book, what ideas or opinions did you have about Buddhism? Now that you know more, were you right? Sometimes religious misunderstandings lead to intolerance, or a lack of acceptance. Fortunately, exchanging knowledge and accurate information creates the opposite effect. Do your part to increase awareness and respect for all religions! Every week, use your research skills to find an interesting fact about Buddhism, Judaism, Christianity, Hinduism, Islam, or Sikhism. Encourage your family members to do the same. Try to set aside time to share what you learn at the dinner table!*

Reaching enlightenment is the goal of Buddhists.

# Think About It

Researchers who study population trends, or patterns, say that the Asia-Pacific region is currently home to about 4 billion people. Remember that 99 percent of the world's 488 million Buddhists live there. The population in this region is predicted to rise to 5 billion by 2050. By that point, however, researchers say that only 486 million people will practice Buddhism worldwide. What do you think this reveals about Buddhism's growth—both in the Asia-Pacific and across the globe? How do you think this compares to population trends for other major world religions?

# For More Information

## FURTHER READING

Blake, Philip. *My Religion and Me: We Are Buddhists*. London: Hachette Children's Books, 2016.

Carew-Miller, Anna. *Buddha: Father of Buddhism*. Broomall, PA: Mason Crest Publishers, Inc., 2014.

Glossop, Jennifer, and John Mantha (illustrator). *The Kids Book of World Religions*. Toronto: Kids Can Press, Ltd., 2013.

## WEB SITES

**The Buddha Center—For Children**
www.thebuddhacenter.org/buddhism-for-children/
Check out this Web site for stories, videos, and coloring sheets related to Buddhism.

**BuddhaNet Kids Page**
www.buddhanet.net/mag_kids.htm
Visit this page for links to songs, stories, and an online program that lets you make your own Buddha picture.

# GLOSSARY

**alms** (AHLMZ) money, clothes, food, and other things given to poor people

**contentment** (kuhn-TENT-muhnt) being peacefully happy; being satisfied with life

**demigods** (DEH-mee-gahdz) beings who are part god and part human

**incense** (IN-sens) a substance that is burned to produce a pleasant smell

**laypeople** (LAY-pee-puhl) people who belong to a religion but are not the leaders

**missionaries** (MISH-uh-ner-eez) people sent out to teach about religion and do good works

**monks** (MUHNGKS) men who live apart from society in a religious community according to strict rules

**morality** (muh-RAL-ih-tee) principles about what is right and wrong that guide your actions

**nobility** (noh-BIL-ih-tee) belonging to a family that is of a very high social class

**rituals** (RICH-oo-uhlz) acts that are always performed in the same way, usually as part of a religious or social ceremony

**Sanskrit** (SANT-skrit) a language that was spoken many years ago in India and is still used in the practices of Buddhism and Hinduism

**sermons** (SUR-muhnz) speeches given during religious services

**yoga** (YOH-guh) a system of exercises and meditation that helps people control their minds and bodies and become physically fit

# INDEX